Healthcare Allocation and
Applying Catholic Social Teaching

Paul Gately
Ashley Beck
David Albert Jones

The Centre for
Bioethics & Emerging
Technologies

The Catholic Truth Society
Publishers to the Holy See

About the Authors

Paul Gately BSc, MA, ARCS, FIA is a Fellow of the Institute of Actuaries who holds an MA in Bioethics from St Mary's University College, Twickenham. Prior to retirement, he held senior management positions in global professional services firms and he is currently in his third year of the Formation Programme for the Permanent Diaconate of the Catholic Church. He is married with two adult children.

Fr Ashley Beck MA is Assistant Priest in the parish of Beckenham in the Archdiocese of Southwark. He is also Dean of Studies of the Permanent Diaconate formation programme for nine Catholic dioceses in southern England and Wales, and is a Visiting Lecturer at St Mary's University College, Twickenham. He is the author of a number of booklets for the Catholic Truth Society and various articles and reviews on Catholic Social Teaching and other topics, and is co-editor of the *New Diaconal Review*. A former Anglican clergyman, he is married with two school age daughters.

Dr David Albert Jones MA, MA, MSt, DPhil, FHEA is the Director of the Anscombe Bioethics Centre, Oxford, Research Fellow in Bioethics at Blackfriars Hall, Oxford, and Visiting Professor in Bioethics at St Mary's University College, Twickenham. He read Natural Sciences and Philosophy at Cambridge, and Theology at Oxford. He is Vice-chair of the Ministry of Defence Research Ethics Committee and is on the National Reference Group of the Liverpool Care Pathway. He is married and lives in Oxford.

Healthcare Allocation and Justice. Centre of Bioethics and Emerging Technologies, St Mary's University College, Waldegrave Road, Strawberry Hill, Twickenham TW1 4SX / The Anscombe Bioethics Centre, 17 Beaumont Street, Oxford OX1 2NA.

Published 2011 by the Incorporated Catholic Truth Society, 40-46 Harleyford Road, Vauxhall, London SE11 5AY. Copyright © 2010 Centre of Bioethics and Emerging Technologies / The Anscombe Bioethics Centre.

Contents

Introduction

The aim of this booklet is to support professionals working in healthcare, especially those in leadership roles, in drawing on the resources of Catholic social teaching and ethics to help facilitate better decision-making in the area of resource allocation. It is the fruit of a project coordinated by the Centre of Bioethics and Emerging Technologies at St Mary's University College in Twickenham together with the Anscombe Bioethics Centre in Oxford. The project has been generously supported by sponsors including the Charles Plater Trust.

The main authors are Paul Gately (Section 1), Fr Ashley Beck (Section 2), and Dr David Albert Jones (Section 3). Each has commented on the others' work and all have benefited from additional comments by Dr Pia Matthews and Dr Stephen Bullivant. The project has also benefited from a number of meetings and interviews with professionals including Jim McManus, Elizabeth Butler, Dr Thomas Mann, Dr Neil Weir, Jolyon Vickers, Fr Nigel Griffin and Helen Booth. It draws on work that others have done before and especially that of Bishop Anthony Fisher and Prof Luke Gormally. We are grateful for the help of these and others in this process, though they have not been directly involved with the drafting and are not responsible for any weaknesses or omissions in the booklet.

Healthcare allocation is a controversial topic. It is not easy to apply principles of justice to the question of how to share out resources when there are not enough to satisfy every possible request. Nevertheless, decisions need to be made and it is imperative that we make decisions justly. The aim of this booklet is to show how Catholic social teaching can be brought to bear on the question of allocation. It should not be seen as a set of answers to this question (even though the last section does pose questions and attempt to give answers). The booklet is critical of what it identifies as utilitarian approaches to allocation. However, no attempt is made to set out in any detail a comprehensive alternative for healthcare allocation to that employed within the healthcare system at present or to the system described in recent Government proposals for the future.

People in good faith will reasonably come to different conclusions from the authors when it comes to particular answers. Rather, the value of this booklet lies more in the example it gives of deliberating about these questions. It invites readers to ask for themselves how to apply the substantive ethical principles of Catholic social teaching to the difficult problems before them.

This booklet is in three sections:

- Section 1 sets out the problem of healthcare allocation in the context of the United Kingdom and draws attention to some particular concerns.

- Section 2 sets out some intellectual resources for addressing this problem: the key principles of Catholic social teaching.

- Section 3 applies these resources to this problem.

The booklet is written to make sense as a whole but the sections each have a slightly different style and are designed to stand in their own right. It does not have to be read in order, or read through in one sitting. Furthermore, we hope the booklet can be used in more than one way. For example, Section 2 can be used as an introduction to Catholic social teaching with the issue of healthcare allocation as an illustrative example. Similarly, the questions in Section 3 could provide an exercise for group discussion on justice and healthcare allocation if, for example, they are given to a group without our proposed answers and then with our answers. However this booklet is used, we hope it provokes thought and discussion and that it helps those who are faced more than ever with difficult decisions on 'who gets what' - when everyone can't have everything.

Section 1: Setting the scene and highlighting some concerns

1.1 Huge pressure on resources

Healthcare and its allocation are subjects that have received a great deal of public attention, particularly in recent years. The system of healthcare operated in the UK has come under increasing pressure as a result of a number of factors:

- Improving longevity and changing demographics;

- Changes in lifestyles;

- The increasing incidences of particular medical conditions;

- Changes in public attitudes to healthcare utilisation;

- Changes in government policy;

- The cumulative effect of healthcare cost inflation brought on by advances in medical technology, well in excess of increases in general price inflation.

The growing recognition within the public consciousness that healthcare expenditure within the UK had persistently lagged behind other countries with well developed economies led the UK Government, on the back of a successful growing economy, to allocate significant additional resources to healthcare so that whereas these comprised 4.5% of GDP in 1989-90, they comprised 7.7% of GDP in 2008-09 and 8.5% of GDP[1] in 2009-10, partly as a result of the UK economy shrinking in that year. At the time of the publication of *Maximising Value For Money in the NHS* in July 2000, the then Health Secretary, Alan Milburn said, 'It is vital in the NHS, as in every public sector organisation, that every penny is spent in the most cost effective manner and to maximise benefits to patients,' (Department of Health 2000:1). These words seem to endorse a utilitarian approach to healthcare allocation. It is also clear that, despite the increase in

---

[1] Table 4.4 HM Treasury PESA 2010 giving estimated outturn

funding, healthcare resources are insufficient for meeting the ever-growing demands. Additionally, the perception exists that the benefits, which were expected have not been realised, so that 'value for money' within the NHS has also become a significant issue for the healthcare authorities.

The Department of Health departmental report 2006 shows that approximately 45% of the NHS Hospital and Community Health Services expenditure in the year 2003-4 was spent on those aged 65 or over, who represented 16% of the population (2006: 104). In their population projections[2], the Office of National Statistics, in addition to highlighting a growing population and improving longevity, shows the percentage of the population expected to be over State Pension Age[3] increasing from 19% in 2008 to 22% in 2033, representing some 4.8 million people, with a corresponding reduction in the 'Working Age to State Pension Age support ratio' to 2.78 from 3.23, a change of 14% in this period. (Two-thirds of the projected increase in the population of 10.2 million over the period is either directly or indirectly (births of immigrants) due to migration, which has a material bearing on these figures since migration is assumed to take place, predominantly, at the younger ages.) That is, other things being equal, over this period and on these projections, the working population may have to support a significant increase in the cost of healthcare for the elderly. The situation will be exacerbated because the number of people at the very oldest ages will increase significantly. For example, those aged 85 and over are expected to more than double from 1.3 million in 2008 to 3.3 million by 2033.

---

[2] Office for National Statistics' 2008-based principal (or central) National population projections available on *www.ons.gov.uk*

[3] State Pension Age is 65 for men and 60 for women. Projections assume the latter will increase uniformly to 65 years over the period 2010 to 2020 and that between 2024 and 2046, State Pension Age will increase in three stages from 65 years to 68 years. The Government has, however, recently announced that the State Pension Age will increase from 65 years for both men and women (now to apply from 2018) to 66 years in 2020.

Furthermore, we have recently experienced a significant deterioration in the world economy, from which the UK has not been spared. At the end of the 2009-10 Financial Year, the public sector net debt (including financial interventions) stood at £893 billion, equivalent to 62% of GDP. During the year, the deficit increased by, approximately, £150 billion, and, on current projections (October 2010), is expected to increase further by a similar level for the Financial Year 2010-11.

In July 2010 the Government published a White Paper entitled 'Equity and excellence: Liberating the NHS' which set out proposals for the most significant changes in the NHS since its inception in 1948. Despite the current economic situation, the White Paper states that health spending will increase in real terms in each year of the lifetime of the present Parliament, but that the NHS will be required to make efficiency savings of some £20 billion over the four years to 2013-14, designed, it says, 'to meet the current financial challenge and the future cost of demographic and technological change' (p. 5). Additionally, management costs within the NHS are to be cut by more than 45% over the same period.

The Government says that it intends to 'radically delayer and simplify the number of NHS bodies and radically reduce the Department of Health's own NHS functions' (p. 5). Strategic Health Authorities and Primary Care Trusts are expected to disappear within three years. The Government will devolve power and responsibility for commissioning services to GPs and their practice teams working in consortia, to the extent that they will be responsible for about 80% of the overall NHS budget which currently stands in excess of £100 billion. A number of doctors have reacted unfavourably to the prospect of assuming this responsibility, something which they feel ill-equipped to manage, and which may well change the way in which the public perceive GPs in the future. The BMA have warned that certain proposals within the White Paper 'would risk shifting the focus onto cost rather than quality' (BMA 2010: 1).

Local authorities will promote the joining up of local NHS services, social care and health improvement. All NHS trusts will become or be part of foundation trusts, which sit outside the NHS and whose freedoms will be expanded, with the 'arbitrary cap' on the amount which they can earn from other sources, for example, from private medicine being removed (p. 36). They are to become part of what the Government states will be 'the largest social enterprise sector in the world' (p. 5). They 'will be regulated in the same way as any other providers, whether from the private or voluntary sector' (p. 36).

Separately, the White Paper champions patient choice so that 'Patients will have choice of any provider, choice of consultant-led team, choice of GP practice and choice of treatment' (p. 3). Success on clinical outcomes is to be measured not through what the Government calls 'bureaucratic process targets' (held by some as being responsible for the fact that nurses now spend as little as one-third of their time with patients) but through measures like disease related survival rates.

An independent NHS Commissioning Board will be established to 'allocate and account for NHS resources, lead on quality improvement... [and] have an explicit duty to promote equality and tackle inequalities in healthcare' (p. 5). The powers of Ministers over day-to-day decisions are to be limited.

Given their radical nature it is difficult to estimate the outcome of these changes with any certainty. Despite the Government's financial commitment to the NHS over the short term, the above clearly demonstrates a poor prospect of being able to meet the growing demand for healthcare and that a number of key decisions with significant implications for some patient groups will have to be made. As a consequence, there may well be major social and political ramifications, compounded by the possible implementation of the radical proposals contained in the White Paper.

1.2   A brief description of the allocation process

Government Departments have to compete for their share of the available resources. In this respect Health is no different from, say, Education or Defence. Any allocation outcome will depend upon a process which is complex, which needs to take into account many factors, and which can be heavily influenced by politics. The outcome decided upon is not a decision based purely on economics; no attempt is made to evaluate, in the most precise economic terms possible, through some cost benefit analysis, the value of the benefits expected to arise from any inter-departmental allocation, with the intention of adopting that allocation which maximises these benefits. As this decision is arguably the most important decision in the entire allocation process, it is well to remember in what follows how it is derived or rather how it is not derived.

At the next level of allocation, we find Primary Care Trusts (PCTs) who currently hold just over 80% of the total NHS budget. They are required to maximise the well being of the population they serve subject to the resources made available to them. The budgets of the PCTs are related to a weighted capitation formula, which is based on the stated principle of enabling PCTs to commission similar levels of care for populations with similar healthcare needs, and to reduce avoidable health inequalities. The formula has changed a number of times over the 30 year period of its existence, with the stated intention of always arriving at a 'fairer' distribution. In addition to the size of the population served by the PCT, allowances are made for age related need and additional need based upon a socio-economic deprivation formula as well as geographical variation in the cost of providing services. As a result, Manchester receives twice the funding per head of population compared to Oxford. In recent times, a separate formula has been introduced to allocate resources to reducing health inequalities. Interestingly, however, there is no requirement falling upon PCTs to spend the allocation according to the basis on which it has been derived. PCTs can commission from a variety of care providers, including NHS and private hospitals and clinics, the voluntary sector and in some cases social services. As mentioned above, the Government has announced proposals to do away with PCTs and to place commissioning within the hands of GPs and their practice teams working in consortia.

The above describes the process at what we might call the macro level of allocation. Together with this, there exists another level of allocation concerned with the approach taken to decide how individual treatments, determined on the basis of clinical benefits and cost considerations, are provided or rejected under the NHS. NICE (National Institute for Health and Clinical Excellence) has been the key decision maker here. NICE was established in 1999 by the UK Government, as part of the NHS, under the name of National Institute for Clinical Excellence. Its website states that NICE is 'the independent organisation responsible for providing national guidance on the promotion of good health and the prevention and treatment of ill health' (*www.nice.org.uk*). Its guidance on what it describes as technology appraisals, covering new pharmaceutical treatments, procedures, devices and diagnostic methods is mandatory. Its guidelines on broader clinical practice relating to treatment for specific diseases and conditions and those on public health are advisory. NICE has operated for a good number of years on this basis. However, Andrew Lansley, the Health Secretary, has now announced his intention to remove the powers held by NICE to ban drugs it considers too expensive, although NICE will still maintain its role in looking at the effectiveness of new drugs and in providing advice in this regard. The Health Minister, Lord Howe, states that 'NICE is recognised as an international leader in the evaluation of drugs and health technologies and it will continue to have an important advisory role, including in assessing the *incremental therapeutic benefits* of new medicines. Its role will increasingly focus on authoritative advice to clinicians on how to deliver the most effective treatments and on the development of quality standards'; these are regarded as being vital for the time when GPs take the lead on commissioning.

In response to this change, Andrew Dillon, Chief Executive of NICE, said 'We support moves to extend access to new treatments at prices which reflect the additional value to patients [*that is, extend beyond clinical effectiveness as part of the introduction of 'value-based pricing' - see 1.6*]. NICE is the global leader in evaluating the benefits of new drugs and we anticipate being at the heart of the new arrangements'. This change is expected to be introduced in 2014; detailed proposals are now awaited.

1.3   Healthcare Economics

In the next two sections we will describe in simplified form how healthcare economists measure health benefits and the cost effectiveness of medical treatment, and how they relate to what Lord Howe calls 'incremental therapeutic benefits'. It is important to understand how these calculations are made in order to appreciate their underlying methodology and assumptions and the way in which they are fair or unfair. For these reasons the reader is encouraged to persevere.

The first step is to create a health profile setting out of a number of domains of health, each with different levels of functionality. These health states, covering disability and distress, are then assigned a utility value between 0 (representing death) and 1 (representing good / best health), called the health related Quality of Life value. This is commonly done by asking patients various questions aimed at obtaining their subjective view for the point at which they are indifferent about the choice between two options; for example, if 15 years of life following a stroke was regarded as 'equivalent' to 9 years with a healthy life (the Quality of Life value for this state of health, in this example, would be 0.6). There is a good deal of subjective measuring in this. In order to cover all the possible health states under consideration, some mathematical modelling is required. This can, however, produce some strange results, with negative Quality of Life values for the states of poorest health, and therefore corresponding, technically, to a position worse than death. NICE, in describing this situation, claims that 'Health states can be considered worse than death and thus have a negative value' (2008: 36). In other words, the quality of life of an individual may be so poor that they are deemed to be better off dead.

Economists have produced a single measure which combines both morbidity and mortality so that they can combine the resulting clinical effectiveness of an intervention with its cost, so as to assess its cost effectiveness. This can then be used when prioritising interventions across different programmes. The measure combines life expectancy with a 'quality of life' factor deemed to represent the actual health of an individual, as produced above, which for one commonly used generic instrument aims to capture physical mobility, self-care, ability to handle daily living, absence of pain and discomfort, and absence of anxiety and depression. The individual's life expectancy, so adjusted, is hereafter referred to in this booklet as their QALY (Quality Adjusted Life Year) status. In the simple example used above, the QALY status for someone following a stroke who has a life expectancy of 15 years is 9 QALYs (15 times 0.6); that is, the equivalent of 9 years in good health.

When assessing clinical effectiveness, the expected QALY status after the intervention (allowing for the probabilities of the various outcomes that can occur) is compared to the QALY status immediately before, so as to determine the increase in the number of QALYs; that is, what the healthcare economist regards as the health benefit gained. If this figure is then divided into the cost figure for the intervention, we arrive at the *cost effectiveness ratio* for the intervention (an indication of its value for money); that is, the cost of acquiring one additional QALY (one extra healthy year). The lower this figure is, (that is, the lower the amount required for gaining one extra healthy year of life), the more attractive the intervention from an economic standpoint. In this scheme of things, this lends itself to maximising health gains derived in this way, as measured by QALYs, for a given cost, so as to meet the objective of achieving better value for money.

1.4   Some criticism of NICE

When comparing a new treatment with an existing one, however, another measure has been used by NICE, the *incremental cost effectiveness ratio*. This is determined by dividing the increase in costs by the increase in QALYs gained by the new treatment over and above the current standard treatment (an example of how this is calculated is set out below). NICE would then judge whether this was acceptable, leading to the new treatment being introduced. NICE, however, has had no absolute threshold and has not directly taken into account the level of overall affordability within the NHS when making these judgements. The House of Commons Health Committee (HOCHC) criticised NICE in this regard, noting in the Summary of its 2007 Report on NICE that, 'The affordability of NICE guidance and the threshold it uses to decide whether a treatment is cost effective is of serious concern[4].' It also said, 'The threshold [*the maximum incremental cost effectiveness ratio permitted* and *generally, taken as between £20,000 and £30,000*] is not based on empirical research... Nor is the threshold directly related to the NHS budget... [however] PCTs appear to use thresholds[5] for treatments not assessed by NICE... lower than the NICE thresholds' (2007: 239-240).

NICE responded to HOCHC by saying that decision taking on the threshold involves a great deal of 'pragmatic thresholdery' which takes into account a 'sympathetic view' of innovation, treatments for cancer, children and patients towards the end of their lives, as well as the severity of the illness, the latter being the subject of a review carried out by the Citizens Council of NICE. (The next edition of NICE's Social Value Judgements (see 1.7) is due to include severity of disease as a factor that NICE and its advisory bodies take into account in their decision taking, although the extent to which this is to be done is not known).

As a result of their approach, NICE could approve a new treatment (N) which has a cost effectiveness ratio (cost per QALY gained) greater than that of the standard treatment (S) currently in use; that is, one that provides poorer value for money, as shown by the following illustration, designed simply to demonstrate the principles involved:

---

[4] This criticism was also made in the Committee's Report on NICE in 2002.
[5] Amounts of £12,000 and £19,000 to gain an extra QALY in circulatory disease and cancer, respectively.

S provides a gain of 4 QALYs at a cost of £50,000. (Cost effectiveness ratio = £12,500). N provides a gain of 6 QALYs and costs £84,000. (Cost effectiveness ratio = £14,000). Incremental cost effectiveness ratio = £17,000 (£34,000÷2), which is within the threshold for approving N, which provides more benefit, although S provides better value for money.

In this situation, despite the additional benefits arising for the patient group directly impacted, a number of important considerations arise when approving a new treatment which has a greater cost than the standard treatment currently in use. When NICE has made a new treatment mandatory, no additional funding has been provided to meet the additional cost which has had to be accommodated within an already determined budget. Also NICE has not recommended the specific cuts that should be made in order to balance the books. Each PCT has therefore had to decide how to do this, and in order to achieve a more cost effective situation overall has had to be certain that it identifies poorer cost effective treatments from which to disinvest. A failure to do so would lead to producing a poorer value for money situation overall.

But there are other consequences to making this decision. The most telling 'cost' falls on those patients on whom disinvestment impacts directly; the gain of others will be their loss. The decision therefore to approve a new and more expensive treatment leads to a revised allocation with potentially significant consequences for those patients who have to forego existing treatments, a scenario which has caused difficulties for the doctors of those patients who must be advised of this change. In the particular case of high profile campaigns fought by the media, it is easy to sympathise with particular individuals made known by the media who would benefit from a new drug, even though its cost well exceeds the NICE 'threshold', a situation which may occur more frequently in the future. Such campaigns have put political pressure on government ministers to reverse decisions and to sanction the introduction of new drugs. The individuals who must now forego their treatment are not so visible to the public eye, but they do most certainly exist. NICE has been divorced from the budgetary process, and taken no part in its ownership, either its construction or delivery. Yet it has made recommendations on new treatments that are mandatory, and at the same time has been spared the consequences of these recommendations in having no direct accountability to those whose treatments have been taken away. As a statement of fact, this is certainly true, but we should also acknowledge that the idea that cost effectiveness should be an integral part of a systematic and explicit process, underpinning the basis for determining which new treatments should be approved, has a great deal of support.

We do however need to be clear about the consequences of what will come in 2014. The Health Secretary, Andrew Lansley, has said that it is now proposed 'to move to an NHS where patients will be confident that where their clinicians believe a particular drug is the right and most effective one for them, then the NHS will be able to provide it for them'. This represents a huge commitment. Yet if drugs will now be approved and provided by doctors for patients that hitherto would have been rejected on the grounds of cost effectiveness, as understood by NICE, this necessarily means that fewer resources will be made available for other patients than would otherwise have been the case. The same problem as that described above remains; indeed, becomes potentially greater in terms of de-selection. The change is not a remedy for meeting the needs of all patients, and GPs and their local consortia will be in the front line for taking these decisions (see also Section 2 of the booklet regarding the principle of subsidiarity within Catholic social teaching). They will be exposed to the power of special interest groups, as will the Government who will negotiate directly with the pharmaceutical companies on price, the basis for which is now to be understood in the context of value-based pricing. The change can be expected to introduce considerable variation in practice across the country.

1.5   Attractions of the QALY

Supporters of the QALY place great store by its objectivity. A QALY gained in one disease is equivalent to a QALY gained in another. The weight given to the gain of a QALY is the same, regardless of how many QALYs are currently enjoyed, how many are in prospect, the age, sex or ethnicity of beneficiaries or their deservingness (that is, there is no penalty where conditions could be regarded as self-inflicted); it is also independent of any deprivation suffered outside health. An additional QALY is regarded as having the same value for all, although that is not the same as saying that a treatment, successfully prescribed for both young and old for a given complaint, will produce the same health gain for each, as understood by healthcare economists. In fact, because of differences in age and hence life expectancy, there may, in this situation, be significant variation in what economists regard as health gains; that is, QALYs gained, even though the state of health of young and old would benefit equally. This is discussed further below.

1.6   Objections to the QALY

Given the importance to NICE which QALYs have as the principal method of health outcome and their likelihood of remaining the basis for determining clinical effectiveness beyond 2014, the claim that QALYs are objective is now examined in some detail. Brock has made a number of significant criticisms and observations (2003: 3-5). These, together with others of the present writer, are set out below:

- QALYs suffer, fatally in the opinion of some, from the inherent problem of incommensurability, i.e. the impossibility of ranking changes in life prolongation with those producing an enhanced 'quality of life', so that measuring health gain in terms of QALYs lacks integrity and is never truly objective.

- Quality of life measures are held to be contentious, misrepresenting what the name suggests, because they fail to allow for cultural, ethnic, social and religious factors and the goods generally required for human flourishing. Indeed, there are likely to be significant mismatches in many cases between values inherent in the QALY and the values placed by individuals on their own health and lives.

- The focus on a single health outcome, even with some statistical appreciation of the uncertainty surrounding the estimates obtained for particular interventions, is too narrow, because several health outcomes will be important; for example, the importance of access to health and social care after leaving hospital, social support and cognitive ability.

- QALYs fail to take into account any benefits other than those relating to clinical effectiveness. The example of the well being of carers in the case of dementia treatments is often cited in this regard. This has been one of the considerations for removing the final say on new drugs from NICE, and the introduction of 'value-based pricing'; the price to be paid for drugs will no longer be based purely on cost effectiveness thresholds set by NICE. When 'value' is considered, the value to patients, carers, and society will also be taken into account.

QALYs are discriminatory because:-

- They reduce the technical capacity for older people to benefit (because of their shorter life expectancy) and this will become hugely significant with the increasing impact of our changing demographic profile: QALY status is clearly heavily dependent on age. Further, Age Concern sees 'chronological age', as opposed to 'physiological age', as being a very poor indicator of risk at a particular level: because heterogeneity in health is known to increase with age, it maintains that a focus on QALY status, based on age-determined life expectancies derived from mortality tables, can seriously misrepresent the prospects of those in old age who are in good health (2005: 2). Additionally, decisions can be made to exclude the elderly from clinical trials even though the elderly take the most medication. As a result, there is no prospect of their being able to satisfy the evidence based test necessary to support their participation in some new healthcare programmes.

- Individuals suffering from a number of conditions can produce a lower QALY gain than those holding a greater pre-treatment QALY status, even though each had the same life expectancy, and even though all benefited equally from a particular treatment (the disability / co-morbidity problem).

- Finally, the way QALYs are used may well inculcate a mindset that serves to compromise beneficence and potentially undermine the doctor-patient relationship. The use of QALYs can encourage a focus on the quality of life so that it can become the only determinant in treatment decisions, as was the situation in the Tony Bland case brought before the courts. Even though he was not dying, his condition was thought to be a life unworthy of living and was described by one law lord as a 'humiliation.' We have already seen how negative utility (quality of life) values are used to describe some health states, which suggests certain implications were demand greatly to exceed the resources available.

There is further contentiousness on a number of other technical aspects of the QALY but these are not included here. The use of QALYs solely to discriminate between treatments for the same patient as opposed to between patients would clearly avoid some of these objections.

1.7   NICE and Social Value Judgements

The impact of some of the issues identified in the above could be reduced, at least in part, by weighting QALYs with so-called equity weights, to produce adjusted QALYs, which would act at the expense of economic efficiency, through some system of preferences based on social value judgements. Policymakers could simply decree priorities. NICE chose, however, to carry out a consultation with healthcare users in 2005 and published its conclusions in December 2005 in the document *Social Value Judgements - Principles for the Development of NICE Guidance*. NICE defines a 'Social Value Judgement' as 'an ethical opinion made either implicitly or explicitly that a particular course of action, institutional arrangement or method of analysis ought to be implemented, or is itself good' (2005: 37). The next section of the booklet explores how these judgements, in terms of both their scope and effect, can be judged in the light of Catholic social teaching.

NICE affirmed that patients should not be denied treatment because of age, gender and sexual orientation, socio-economic status, race, self inflicted conditions and conditions associated with stigma (2005: 22). This is a conspicuously weak statement, particularly since NICE says nothing explicitly about the differences in treatment received between, for example, the old and frail compared to younger members of society with similar conditions.

1.8 Social Value Judgements - How NICE views particular ethical theories

NICE considered various ethical theories of distributive justice when carrying out this exercise. When looking at utilitarianism and egalitarianism, it stated that 'Each...articulates ideas that most would be reluctant to relinquish and where one theory is weak, the other is often strong and some compromise has to be found' (2005: 13). Again, this is a very weak statement, since it offers no basis for determining how such judgements are to be made. NICE commented that 'Egalitarians seek healthcare to be distributed, so far as possible, so that each person can achieve a fair share of the opportunities available in a particular society' (2005: 12).

NICE described 'The traditional paternalistic approach' as being based on the 'need principle' where priorities are set on the basis of clinical need, and how this has been largely based on 'the premise of doctor knows best' (2005: 12). To conflate these matters is misleading, since the principle of allocation in accordance with need does not depend upon a paternalistic approach. NICE went on to dismiss the principle, since it 'takes no account of other issues' (these are not cited), and because it offers 'no solution relating to a healthcare system as a whole' (2005: 12). Addressing need, though it might not be possible always fully to meet it, is readily identified as fundamental to Christian values and has been for some two thousand years, but is rejected by NICE as a governing principle of healthcare. Perversely, NICE called the principle the 'Marxist approach to distributive justice' (2005: 12). The effect, and perhaps the motivation, of this label is to discredit the need principle by association, since Marx's social, political and economic policies are now largely discredited. Additionally, however, with the advance of secularism, religion is increasingly seen as a private matter having no place in public policy; undoubtedly, this can have implications for how human beings are regarded and how healthcare is allocated, which may run contrary to how Catholic teaching understands the human person and our duty to care for one another.

Although acknowledging that equity lies at the heart of the NHS, NICE regarded much of the philosophical literature on equity as being far from applicable in the real world and therefore unhelpful. As a result, NICE argued that it was forced to make its own judgements. These include the stated objective of removing the so called 'postcode lottery,' that is, avoiding local variations in affordability impacting upon healthcare. However this not been achieved and local PCT disinvestment decisions, which are in part a response to cost pressures sanctioned by NICE, have contributed to these variations. Arguably, such variations may well increase given the proposals under the White Paper and the proposed change to remove from NICE the final say in deciding whether a new treatment should be introduced.

1.9   Second edition of Social Value Judgements

In July 2008, NICE issued a second edition of *Social Value Judgements*. Under Principle 3, NICE proposed to recognise 'the need to distribute health resources in the fairest way within society as a whole' but fell well short of providing an explicit description of what fairness means and therefore how the 'fairest way' can hope to be identified and established (2008: 18). It stated that within the QALY formula 'Balancing life years gained and quality involves social value judgements, some of which may be very difficult to make' (2008: 17). Finally, under Principle 8, it proposed that NICE 'should actively target health inequalities, including those associated with sex, age, race, disability and socioeconomic status' (2008: 28). No proposals were made as to how this was to be achieved or even whether specific targets were to be set, but it is clear that such an objective is crucial to most people's concept of fairness, indeed to the very purpose of healthcare itself. There exists a glaring tension between the use of the QALY formula, which was again championed, and the objective of reducing health inequality associated with age and disability.

Utility and justice provide competing measures for allocating scarce resources. NICE makes the case that neither should exclusively dictate the approach to healthcare. There does seem however to be a striking imbalance in favour of utility because of the QALY formula and the effect of NICE's current stance on social value judgements. The Department of Health describes its purpose as being to 'improve the health and wellbeing of people in England'. Given the econometrics that have been deployed in allocation decisions, it is tempting to conclude that the essential good in healthcare has been expressed principally in overall terms, with the key objective being to maximise the return from the available resources; little prominence has been given to the question of how this can adversely affect particular individuals within certain groups in society. This objective has been defended on the grounds that it provides the highest healthcare return to the taxpayer, and is fully supported by mathematical economics; however, from what we have seen above, it can hardly be described as constituting a precise science.

QALYs, because of the way they are applied, can seriously prejudice the interests of significant minorities because of a technically imposed incapacity to benefit. Indeed, Fisher and Gormally, following their review of QALYs, say that the logic of utilitarian approaches, as demonstrated by the use of the QALY, favours a policy that gives the lowest priority to 'the terminally ill, dying, elderly, chronically sick or incapacitated, severely handicapped, and permanently unconscious', (2001: 65) even to the point of elimination.

There are opportunities under the Government's proposal to introduce 'value-based pricing' to address some of the objections to QALYs, but, again, we need to remember that removing these does not increase the amount of available resources.

1.10   Need and personal responsibility

It is a pity that NICE treated the need principle so dismissively, since seeing need as the governing principle does not, for example, lead to satisfying every desire anyone may have to improve their functioning, or to accepting the position of the vitalist, namely, that of sustaining life at all costs whilst one has the means to do so. Furthermore, is it reasonable, for example, always to try and improve the level of functioning of someone who is already operating at a high level, if there are only sufficient resources to meet greater needs?

In responding to need, personal responsibility, like preventative medicine, is likely to become an increasingly important issue in allocation in the future. John Reid, as Secretary of State for Health, said in 2004, 'We can provide the opportunities, we can provide the incentive, but real people engaged in the hard work of changing their own lives make the difference'. If people can be helped to adopt lifestyles, encouraged by incentives and other means, that allow them to improve their well-being and reduce the burden falling upon the healthcare system, then this will serve the common good, and limited healthcare resources will be able to stretch that much further.

1.11 Rationalised discrimination - Proposals which would adversely impact the elderly

For some, however, QALYs do not go far enough. While QALYs inherently involve bias against older patients, the economist Alan Williams, would give even less weighting to QALYs at older ages. He describes 'age as an indicator ... of declining capacity to benefit from healthcare' and, in the case of the elderly, asks if life threatening conditions should always take priority over other conditions, since they often involve 'high tech interventions' which can be very expensive (1997: 2). One may readily accept that some needs are untreatable, while treatments for others may be too burdensome or indeed very expensive and achieve little. However, individual situations should be matters requiring a judgement of the particular circumstances: treatment should not be automatically denied because some age limit has been exceeded. Williams, however, advocates such an approach regarding life saving interventions with his concept of a 'fair innings'. His 'fair innings' corresponds to a pre-determined age limit on the demands we can all make for 'keeping us going a bit longer', although Williams fails to clarify what 'a bit longer' means precisely, or the length of a 'fair innings' itself and whether or not this should differ between men and women (1997: 2) He maintains that it reflects 'the biblical view of our life as three score and ten' (1997: 3). However, any claim that the Bible is literally setting a natural limit to one's lifespan, valid for all time, borders on the ridiculous.

Conspicuously, Williams make no appeal to life expectancy, calculated in accordance with the latest known data and based upon actuarial projections. Yet opponents of the 'fair innings' argument can reasonably ask - how would the limit vary with improving longevity? If the limit were to increase then clearly it could prejudice any existing balance between 'acceptable' demand and the supply of resources and leave a greater problem to solve. If it remains fixed, then more people will be brought into the net and the idea of a natural age limit becomes increasingly in conflict with the observable data and its original rationale, so that it becomes an arbitrary ceiling for curtailing demand to the 'sustainable' level. It perhaps serves the supporters of the concept to keep such a limit ill-defined. Their objective is nevertheless clear; namely, to reduce significantly the amount of healthcare provided to the elderly.

The philosopher John Hardwig goes much further, by raising the concept of 'the duty to die'. He maintains that the greater the burden to, and inability to make a positive contribution to, one's family, the greater is the duty to die. This is easily extended beyond the elderly. He says 'A duty to die becomes greater as you get older...To have reached the age of, say, seventy five or eighty years without being ready to die is a moral failing, the sign of a life out of touch with life's basic realities' (2000: 344). There seems here to be a deliberate attempt to confuse having the moral courage to accept a natural death with being under an obligation to have one's life prematurely curtailed. It is not too difficult to see how such a duty could become a requirement: volunteers first, to be then followed by conscripts. Christine Overall criticises Hardwig's proposed duty to die. She says that 'those who are most likely to have a duty to die will be those who have already been deprived throughout their lifetimes; the poor, the unemployed, those with mental and physical disabilities and those who have suffered other disadvantages' (2003: 82).

More recently, Baroness Warnock has said in an interview with the magazine of the Church of Scotland, *Life and Work*, 'If you're demented, you're wasting people's lives, your family's lives and you're wasting the resources of the National Health Service. I've just written an article called *"A Duty to Die?"*'... suggesting that there's nothing wrong with feeling you ought to do so for the sake of others as well as yourself' (cited by Christian Institute: 2008).

1.12 'Culture change' needed in caring for the elderly

It is worth taking particular note of the conclusions and recommendations appearing in the *Joint Committee on Human Rights - Eighteenth Report*, published in July 2007, which investigated the treatment of older people in hospitals and care homes. In its Summary, the Joint Committee referred to 'concerns about poor treatment, neglect, abuse, discrimination and ill considered discharge,' and considered that 'an entire culture change is needed' (2007: 3). It regretted 'the failure of the Department of Health and the Ministry of Justice to give proper leadership and guidance to providers of health and residential care on the implications of the Human Rights Act' (2007: 3). It also recommended that 'NICE should take clearer account of the Convention rights of any patients affected by its decisions on clinical practice' (2007: 3). This lack of direction, at the highest levels, not only indicates the absence of any sense of responsibility, but also, and more worryingly, reveals an astonishing lack of care for this group of vulnerable people. The National Audit Office in its report *End of Life Care*, published in November 2008, confirmed the validity of these criticisms and made a number of recommendations for the Department of Health, for PCTs, the General Medical Council and the Nursing and Midwifery Council.

Given the increasing demands on existing healthcare resources, the very difficult situation in which the UK economy finds itself, the projections regarding future demographics, the effect of the QALY and the overt discrimination against the elderly, which seems to be increasing, we urgently need a culture change in care for the elderly. Such a change can only occur through a rediscovery of the fundamental human values that underpin society. The second section of this booklet examines the key elements of Catholic social teaching, which offers a rich resource not only in relation to reforming the care of the elderly but also in relation to healthcare allocation in general.

Section 2: Catholic social teaching and healthcare allocation

Catholic teaching offers a great deal of help for people working in healthcare who have responsibilities for the allocation of resources. Some of this is what theologians call 'common morality', relating to well-known positions on bioethical issues. Some of it is the body of doctrine and practice known as *Catholic social teaching*. Much of what has been written in this area has not been readily accessible to healthcare professionals in this country and the purpose of this section is to distil elements of the tradition. Moreover some of what has been written took shape at a much earlier stage in the process of reforms in the National Health Service in Britain; so in 2010 we may be in a position to assess how these changes have worked out, especially as drastic new reforms are about to be implemented.

2.1 First principle: The dignity of the human person

This is a foundational principle of Catholic teaching; everything which we want to say about the right way in which patients should be treated within the healthcare system rests on the human dignity of those patients. People know the clear positions of the Catholic Church on what we call *bioethical issues* - questions relating to healthcare such as abortion, IVF, embryo experimentation, human cloning, assisted suicide, euthanasia and so on. Some are critical of the Church because it seems too much concerned only with these issues; while others appear to think the Church should focus only on these issues. However, just as it is the dignity of the human person, created in the image of God, which should safeguard the person's life in the womb and at the end of natural life; so also it is that dignity which determines our attitude to the human person's needs during life, including his or her educational, economic and healthcare needs.

Our dignity as human persons is not negotiable. 'Catholic reflection upon the appropriate level and allocation of healthcare begins with the claim that every human being has intrinsic, equal and inalienable dignity or worth, deserving uncompromising reverence and respect.' (Fisher and Gormally 2001: 147) Our model for this reverence for the human person's health care needs is Jesus himself, who makes manifest the coming of his kingdom through his miracles of physical healing in the gospels - in Mark's gospel particularly these miracles are seen as the battleground of the conflict between good and evil. The Church in its pastoral care for the sick and disabled has sought to model itself on Jesus' healing ministry. We try to reverence the human person in the same way as Jesus did.

The violation of human life within the health system bears out the importance of the dignity of the human person as a foundational principle. The person is fully human from the time before birth to the natural end of his or her mortal life. As Gately (2008) and Jones (2009) have pointed out, some contemporary theories of the person are not only gravely inadequate but positively dangerous as a basis for healthcare decisions. This is already seen in relation to abortion, but is now also threatening in the treatment of some after they have been born. This can be seen implicitly (and sometimes overtly) whenever an elderly person with Alzheimer's is not given the respect due to human persons - if for example his or her healthcare needs are not taken seriously or even his or her need for food and water. Poor care is always a failure to acknowledge the dignity of the patient as a person.

On the basis of this teaching about the dignity of the human person, the Catholic Church has developed an extensive theory of human rights. It is more robust than corresponding secular human rights theories in that it rest upon the Christian doctrine of creation and the dignity and equality of all human beings as made in the image of God (*Genesis* 1.26). The Church's list of human rights is also more extensive than secular counterparts. Pope Blessed John XXIII, in his encyclical letter on peace in the world, *Pacem in Terris,* written shortly before his death from cancer in 1963, wrote: 'Man has a right to live. He has a right to bodily integrity and to the means necessary for the proper development of life, particularly food, clothing, shelter, medical care, rest, and finally, the necessary social services. In consequence, he has the right to be looked after in the event of ill-health, disability and old age.' (Section 11) The vision expressed in chapter 9 of the book of Genesis shows that the sacredness of life, of 'life-blood', means that a right is conferred but also a responsibility: humans are held to account before God for themselves and for others.[6] The Catholic understanding of the right to healthcare cannot be detached from the notion of stewardship and the duty to care responsibly for our health.

What is the level of healthcare to which people have a right? The US Catholic bishops defined this some years ago as 'that healthcare which is necessary and suitable for proper development and maintenance of life' (USCC 1981, Section 11), but there are always likely to be many interpretations. In Britain today these interpretations are going to be affected by cutbacks in resources.

There is another side to the Church's theory of rights: we should not always exercise them. The *Compendium of the Social Doctrine of the Church* quotes Pope Paul VI's letter *Octagesima Adveniens*: 'The more fortunate should *renounce* some of their rights so as to place their goods more generously at the service of others' (2005: para. 158). This voluntary renunciation of rights corresponds to the need to set limits to forms of medical research and treatment which can take away resources which should be used for basic health provision for others. For Catholics one of the most important teaching documents on morality of the 20th century was the Second Vatican Council's Pastoral Constitution on the Church in the Modern World, *Gaudium et Spes,* issued at the close of the Council in December 1965. The constitution says at one point: 'We experience ourselves as creatures subject in many ways to limits... We must repeatedly and unavoidably make choices from the many possibilities that call to us - choosing this option and foregoing those other options.' (Section 10)

---

[6] 'I will demand an account of your life-blood. I will demand an account from every beast and from man. I will demand an account of every man's life from his fellow men.' (*Genesis* 9.5)

The American theologian John Glaser writes of 'powerful forces' which increase the consumption of resources, at least in the American context, in ways which detract from the provision of basic services to some - these include the growing identification of healthcare with technology, the emphasis on 'freedom of choice' by 'providers and consumers', the ways in which the free market and profit operate, and an aversion to control. If we want to expand access to basic care we need an 'effective restraint on health care's expansive dynamic' (Dwyer 1994). This is even more true with regard to inequalities on a global scale: 'Our social teaching challenges developed nations to move beyond narrow pursuit of ever-loftier national health status while millions perish globally for lack of the most primitive care' (Dwyer 1994:442). The Christian concept of responsible stewardship in relation to property ownership is helpful. Scientific knowledge is like any other gift from God and it has to be used responsibly and for the benefit of all: John Paul II in his encyclical *Evangelium Vitae* called for 'a just international distribution of medical resources' (1995: 26, see also Benedict XVI 2009: 9, 26; Jones 2010). At the same time, there can be a tension between renouncing a right and exercising good stewardship of oneself.

2.2   Second principle: The preferential option for the poor

In the 1960s and 1970s one of the most influential theological movements in the Catholic world was what we now call the *theologies of liberation.* Originating in Latin America, this tradition was a sustained reaction to the sufferings of the poor and oppressed, and explored new ways of interpreting the scriptures and the Christian tradition. Although the movement has been controversial, and the Holy See has criticised some tendencies within the tradition, one key concept has become a mainstream Catholic belief. This is the *preferential option for the poor* - an assertion that in human history the Christian God is on the side of the poor and the oppressed, and poses a challenge and judgement to the rich and powerful. The theologians of liberation did not invent the concept. We can see it first of all in the ways which God's justice is portrayed in the Bible - justice on behalf of the widow, the orphan, the stranger, the 'little people' (*anaw'im*) in the Old Testament prophets. We see it too in the assertion of the gospels that God works through the weak and poor and loves them because they, unlike the strong and the rich, know that they are dependent on God, that their hope rests in him. Furthermore, the whole modern tradition of social teaching beginning with Pope Leo XIII's encyclical *Rerum Novarum* draws on this when it calls for workers to receive just wages and decent working conditions.

The American Catholic bishops have written: 'Catholic healthcare should distinguish itself by service to and advocacy for those people whose social condition puts them at the margins of our society and makes them particularly vulnerable to discrimination: the poor, the uninsured and the underinsured; children, the unborn, single parents and the elderly; those with incurable diseases and chemical dependencies; and racial minorities, immigrants and refugees. In particular, the person with mental or physical disabilities, regardless of the cause or severity, must be treated as a unique person of incomparable worth, with the same right to life and to adequate healthcare as all other persons.' (*Ethical and Religious Directives* 1994) This categorisation is as helpful here in the United Kingdom as in the American context.

One category in this list deserves special attention in Britain - immigrants and refugees. For many years the Church in this country has been at the forefront of efforts to provide support for refugees and asylum seekers in the face of press-sponsored bigotry, the activities of groups like the BNP and punitive government legislation. Proper access to health services by refugees and asylum seekers is a major issue for those working to support these most vulnerable members of society: Catholics and others in healthcare have a particular role to play in this (Bishops of England and Wales 2008; Pontifical Council for the Pastoral Care of Migrants and Itinerant People 2004).

The concept of the preferential option for the poor challenges policy makers, and this means that the Church should challenge the dogmatic introduction of market forces into a healthcare setting where this militates against the poorest in society.[7] Many think that spending constraints will have a serious effect on the NHS in terms of patient care and the jobs of employees who are already in many cases amongst the lowest paid; in this harsh environment Catholic decision-makers will need to have clear principles.

2.3   Third principle: The common good and solidarity

Christians in this country began to learn about the concept of the 'Common Good' in late 1996 when the Bishops of England and Wales published their pre-election teaching document of the same name. It was clear that until then the vast majority of Catholics had never encountered the Church's social teaching. What does the concept mean for health care? Two writers on bioethics have written: 'These demands of the common good concern... the provision of basic services to all, some of which are at the same time basic human rights: food, clothing, work, education and access to culture, transportation, basic health care...' (Ashley and O'Rourke 1994: 84) The *Compendium* makes it clear (160ff.) that the common good is a regulative theological principle which must be guaranteed by the State; legislators should 'interpret the common good of their country not only according to the guidelines of the majority but also according to the effective good of all the members of the community, including the minority' (169). This emphasis is particularly important for healthcare resource decisions: often those who need treatment most are those who are less articulate in expressing their needs and winning their case. As Fisher and Gormally put it, the common good 'requires fellowfeeling, genuine self-giving, joint effort with others to promote the flourishing of all, encouragement and support for the efforts of others, and various interventions by the state in accordance with a just hierarchy of values' (2001: 154).

---

[7] For a detailed critique of the free market model in healthcare see Fisher and Gormally (2001: 27ff.) With regard to choice in the NHS, and anxieties expressed about the attitude of the new coalition Government, see the interview with the head of the King's Fund, Chris Ham, *'Scholarly Advice'*, Society Guardian 9th June 2010. See also responses from the fund to the White Paper and their 'Quality in a Cold Climate' project, all detailed on *www. kingsfund.org.uk.*

Provision of healthcare by the community is an expression of the theological virtue of *solidarity*. This sees care for our neighbour as not simply an example of charity or kindness, but as giving others what is their due, in justice; and it is seeing the other as 'an other' - Pope John Paul II made it clear that it is much more than a 'vague feeling of compassion' (John Paul II 1987: 38). Over and against theories about healthcare provision which minimise the role of the State and place too much faith in 'free-market' forces, the place of solidarity makes it clear that ensuring healthcare provision is part of what the state is for.

'Distributive justice' has played an important part in discussions about how healthcare should be resourced. After looking at secular models of distributive justice Fisher and Gormally put forward this test of how it might be judged in healthcare: *'Would I think the healthcare budget and its distribution was fair if I (or someone I loved) were in healthcare need, especially if I were among the weakest in the community (i.e. sick with a chronic, disabling and expensive ailment, elderly, poor and illiterate)? Would I think it were fair if I were one who would go without under the proposed arrangements?* This approach is strongly supported by Jesus' own enunciation of the Gold Rule (*Matthew* 7.12), his explication of its radical demands in the Sermon on the Mount (e.g. *Matthew* 5.40-42; 6.2-4; cf. 10.8), and his repeated insistence on the duties of those with power and wealth to redistribute to the poor and to see things from their perspective (e.g. *Matthew* 19.23-26; *Luke* 6.24; 12.16-21; 16.19-31)' (Fisher and Gormally 2001: 155). So a concomitant reaction would be: 'I would not like to be in that position so therefore I should not let anyone else be.' This theological vision accords with purely secular evidence which shows that people want healthcare resources to be allocated fairly and with special attention to the needy and the poor (Reeves 2000).

How can healthcare be used to reduce inequalities in society? Thirty years ago the *Black Report* looked at data illustrating the fact that ill health and mortality were closely related to social class; other studies have looked at significant inequalities within social classes and income groups. It is not the case that the poorer you are, the less healthy you will be: for example, when the NHS was founded more people in the professional and managerial classes had stress-related ailments such as coronary disease and angina than poorer people; similarly since the NHS was created mortality rates among unskilled manual workers aged over 55 have actually increased and remained high despite an increase in income (Bartley 2004: 3, 7). Evidence from elsewhere in Europe shows that health inequalities are still higher in countries in northern Europe where health and welfare provision is very good than in southern European countries.[8]

2.4 Fourth principle: Subsidiarity

'A community of higher order should not interfere in the internal life of a community of a lower order, depriving the latter of its functions, but rather should support it in the case of need and help co-ordinate its activity with the activities of the rest of society, always with a view to the common good.' (John Paul II 1991: 48) This is the principle of *subsidiarity* which has been important in Catholic social teaching particularly since the 1930s - the need to carry out functions, as far as possible, at the lowest level, the one nearest the people involved.

We can take this further and see how each one of us should show good stewardship of ourselves - of our health. St. Paul tells the Thessalonians, 'If anyone will not work, let him not eat' (2 *Thessalonians* 3.10). To take responsibility for one's own health is also important for fulfilling one's duties to others. After the immediate concern with one's own health, personal responsibility extends to making a contribution to looking after dependants, as well as 'neighbours', a term which, as Jesus makes clear, should be understood broadly or inclusively (*Luke* 10.29 ff.). This neighbourliness is very evident in many cultures, but sadly, seems to be in decline in the United Kingdom.

---

[8] Bartley (2004: 169ff.). The discrepancy is due to differences in diet and climate. In terms of spending on healthcare this is similar to the findings of the recent report from the Nuffield Trust *Funding and Performance of Healthcare Systems in the Four Countries of the UK Before and After Devolution.*

Ashley and O'Rourke write that subsidiarity in healthcare 'provides that charity begins at home, that is, those closest to us and whose need is best known to us should be cared for first.' (1994: 123) In the early days of the NHS and when similar reforms were planned in Ireland, some Catholics claimed that wide-ranging state provision would take functions and responsibilities away from families and this is part of the present debate in the United States. Decision-making in relation to the healthcare needs or perceived needs of family members remains a controversial issue (e.g. over contraceptive advice to teenagers) and increasingly this applies to older relatives for whom we are responsible.

Subsidiarity is also important because of the widespread decentralisation of decision-making over resources in the NHS which has happened since the 1990s. In recent years local Primary Care Trusts have taken important decisions about resource allocation and have bought services from health providers such as hospitals; local GP surgeries have far greater financial autonomy than in the past. This is set to increase dramatically if the new White paper is implemented. In theory, such bodies - both the PCTs and the new consortia of surgeries - are or will be responsive to local needs and the views of local people and are accountable to them. Catholics in healthcare will have differing views about how well this has worked in practice, but we can all recognise that at least at first sight this accords with the principle of subsidiarity.

However there are at least two problems with the way this has happened in terms of Church teaching. The first is that such decentralisation lacks integrity if it is simply a way of enabling the central authority which has given up responsibility to cut costs and resources, placing the lower units in an impossible position by depriving them of the money they need to carry out their tasks - and making them take the blame. The financial realities of this following the White Paper were examined earlier in this booklet (Section 1.1 above). The second problem, which is very urgent in the light of the new White Paper, is that if financial decisions are taken by those with *medical* responsibilities; that is, doctors, then the real needs of patients may not be properly addressed.

The principle of *patient need* is a key way to guide decision-making, and this is obscured if the clinician is also taking financial decisions. Gately writes: 'The structure and organisation of the NHS seems to be moving ever closer to that of a well recognised commercial business model that expresses the belief that profitability and the effective use of resources is maximised by devolving profit centre accountability to the lowest level of the business that can satisfy the required competency requirements. One has seen general practitioners become budget holders...' (Gately 2008: 35)

Of course, it is likely that surgeries, or groups of surgeries, will have to buy the services of people with financial and business expertise - to manage their budgets and ensure good value for money over procurement decisions. Presumably many of these professionals will be men or women who have worked in PCTs or in other parts of the health service and will have valuable experience; but others may not, and will come rather from the world of business, with 'free market' attitudes which in terms of Christian teaching may be at odds with how healthcare should be provided. A lot will depend on the vision and ideals of doctors themselves: given the professional pressures under which they already labour, ensuring that business managers and finance directors behave in the right way may be difficult. Although the details of the White Paper's proposals are still being worked out, many GPs have expressed their reservations about the new powers which are to be given to them. The official reactions of both the public service union UNISON (2010) and the British Medical Association bear this out - the BMA has reiterated its opposition to 'the commercialisation and active promotion of a market approach to the NHS' (BMA 2010:1).

There is another angle. The personalist ethic espoused by Dorothy Day, Peter Maurin and the Catholic Worker (Beck 2008: 30ff.; Day 1997: 178ff.) would see care for those in need as being something the disciples of Christ should simply do themselves - not handing over responsibility to the State or other agencies. There may well be situations, particularly if public funding is to be cut back, where such

Christian initiatives form what this tradition would call 'communities of resistance'. Hans-Martin Sass has argued that subsidiarity and personal responsibility are more important now in healthcare because the traditional concept of solidarity, important in most healthcare systems in Europe, is now more limited. He puts forward a new *triad* of the three ideas of responsibility, solidarity and subsidiarity as a more realistic basis for policy (Sass 1995). Some might argue that Sass concedes too much in his claim that solidarity and the redistribution model has 'lost its moral authority', but the need for balance between the three ideas is clear. So subsidiarity needs handling with care. Nearly twenty years after the beginning of decentralisation in the NHS, we need to analyse how far subsidiarity has worked. Has the decentralisation been authentic in terms of Christian teaching? Will the new decentralisation envisaged by the While Paper be authentic?

2.5   The model of the Good Samaritan

In addition to these key principles of Catholic social teaching, the Gospel provides an exemplary model for healthcare allocation in the parable of the Good Samaritan (*Luke* 10.25-37). Jesus' parable offers a simple picture of one human being responding to the clear needs of another. Like the actions of the man in the parable, health systems can symbolise values in wider society - and these should be 'generosity, respect for the dignity and equality of persons, for the inviolability of human life and the good of health, special concern for the vulnerable and powerless, solidarity with and compassion for those who suffer...Thus health systems can tell the story of the kind of people we are and wish to be.' (Fisher and Gormally 2001: 159)

This seems to imply a 'needs-based' approach to decisions on healthcare resources: '...healthcare should be allocated according to need, irrespective of factors such as race, religion, social contribution, age, consciousness, intelligence, quality of life, provider-whim and ability to pay' (2001: 158). The *caveat* to the strict application of this approach is a preference in favour of the disadvantaged, in line with the concept of the option for the poor, the vulnerable and the marginalised. We might also add that, bearing in mind individual responsibility, it is reasonable to allocate in a way that gives an incentive for people to take responsibility for their own health.

In Section 1 we set out the problem of healthcare allocation in the context of the United Kingdom. In the present Section we have set out some intellectual resources for addressing this problem: the basic principles of Catholic social teaching and the model of the Good Samaritan. The following section will apply these resources to this problem. It is set out as a series of questions and answers in order to bring out as clearly as possible some of the implications of this tradition. It does not aim to be comprehensive but through a series of questions and answers to introduce a way of thinking.

Section 3: Healthcare allocation - applying the principles in practice

3.1   Is rationing unavoidable in healthcare?

Can we avoid difficult allocation decisions in which some patients suffer?

From the analysis in Section 1 it seems impossible to avoid difficult allocation decisions, in the sense of decisions which will leave some possible health benefits unrealised. Despite the increase in funding, it is clear that healthcare resources are insufficient for meeting the ever-growing demands. This is due, among other things, to:

• Improving longevity and changing demographics;

• Changes in lifestyles;

• The increasing incidences of particular medical conditions;

• Changes in public attitudes to healthcare utilisation;

• Changes in government policy;

• The cumulative effect of healthcare cost inflation brought on by advances in medical technology, well in excess of increases in general price inflation.

Can being more efficient resolve the allocation problem?

If the extent of the problem as identified in Section 1 is correct then being more efficient on its own will never 'free up' enough resources to 'solve' the problem of allocation, in the sense of our being able to provide every possible healthcare benefit. Nevertheless, being more efficient is an important element of the moral response to allocation decisions. Even were there more than enough resources, the duty of stewardship would remain. If resources are scarce then we have a greater responsibility to use resources effectively. Finding efficiency savings is a moral imperative. Nevertheless, 'efficiency' needs to be understood broadly and to be pursued in conjunction with other fundamental human values, especially solidarity and justice.

Can spending more resolve the allocation problem?

There may be a case for spending more on a particular discipline or area where the need is increasing or where it has historically been neglected. There may also be a case for increasing the overall amount of spending on healthcare relative to other parts of the economy. Nevertheless, the question must always be asked - where does this money come from? If healthcare gets more, what gets less? And if the overall healthcare budget is not increased then giving more to one area (e.g. cancer care) means giving less to other areas (e.g. mental health).

What are the consequences of a failure to accept the limitations of healthcare resources?

Rationing is inevitable and if this is not acknowledged honestly it will still occur but with less transparency and more unfairness. Lack of public acknowledgement of the need to ration resources will also make people less willing to take more responsibility for health, to pay more, or to forgo unnecessary treatment, though these and other burdens may need to be shared for the sake of the common good. The current financial constraints should help make the inevitability of this even clearer. However, the danger is that in harsh circumstances people will focus more energy on defending their own area of concern to the detriment of those who are in greater need.

3.2 What are the ethical principles of healthcare allocation?

What is the most fundamental ethical principle in allocation?

The most fundamental ethical principle in allocation is the foundational principle of Catholic social teaching, set out in Section 2: the dignity of each and every human person. This key principle provides the measure for all other principles. In Catholic social teaching human dignity is based on the fact that every person is created in the image and likeness of God, even if this dignity may be unrecognised by society. The dignity is equally present in every human being. Nevertheless, a further principle of Catholic social teaching is that preference should be shown to the poor, the vulnerable and the marginalised. This is because it is precisely these people whose dignity is most likely to be overlooked. It is not generally the dignity of the powerful that is under threat.

What other principles of Catholic social teaching are relevant to allocation?

As outlined in section 2, the Catholic understanding of social action rests on the dignity of the human person. The common good of society includes respect for the person. In the Catholic understanding, human beings were created to flourish as social beings and to seek a common good. This social aspect of human beings implies the need for a positive commitment to solidarity. This is very different from the libertarian view of fairness as non-interference, where it would be compatible with this understanding of fairness to abandon the vulnerable. The evaluation of any system of allocation should therefore begin by considering its impact on the most vulnerable.

Can the allocation problem be resolved by democratic processes or other decision making mechanisms?

Public participation in allocation decisions, at least at the macro level, is important to overcome vested interests and to reflect the fact that these decisions result in benefits, costs and other burdens spread across society. Nevertheless, democratic process on its own does not guarantee justice. Indeed public pressure (whether directly through consultations or enquiries or indirectly through the media and lobbying politicians) can easily compromise justice and the common good. Majorities may be unfair to minorities and vocal and active minorities may be unfair to other minorities and/or to the majority. Reflection on allocation decisions should aim at making principled decisions that are fair and best serve the common good. Some of the tools used by NICE were criticised in Section 1. Typically, the QALY and other mechanisms aim to maximize overall health benefit in the population, whereas they should prioritise justice and the needs of the most vulnerable. Nevertheless, NICE at least represents an attempt to be open about rationing and to establish objective and transparent criteria.

3.3 How can one identify what is fair or just in healthcare?

Can Catholic social teaching help us identify what is fair?

As set out in Section 2, the prime rule of fairness is to treat others as you would wish to be treated yourself. This is sometimes referred to as the Golden Rule and is cited by Jesus as a key element of justice (*Matthew* 7.12). In relation to healthcare this requires being honest about limits and then asking whether a proposed pattern of distribution would be fair for all those involved. It is generally easier to detect unfairness than fairness, so it is useful to ask - would this mechanism or pattern of distribution be seen as fair from the perspective of different patient groups including people of different ages? Would it be fair to carers and to professionals? Would it be fair to tax-payers? It is helpful here to follow the advice of the philosopher John Rawls and ask, if you did not know what position you have in society, whether you would consider this a fair system.

Is it fair to give younger patients priority over older patients?

In general, no. People have different needs at different times of their lives. On average people who are older have more health problems and more need for healthcare than those who are younger. It is only fair to provide more healthcare for people who need it more. Nevertheless, it is not only Alan Williams (1997 - see Section 1 above) who has put forward a 'fair innings' argument. The bioethicist Daniel Callahan has seen in modern medicine a failure to accept mortality, a failure that leads to aggressive, burdensome, and wasteful overtreatment. He and others have argued that, all other things being equal, older people at the frontier of a 'reasonable life span' should have a lower priority in healthcare than younger people (Callahan 1990: 153). However, the prioritising of younger over older patients stands in contradiction to the principles of Catholic social teaching. The so called 'fair innings' approach is unfair and indeed dangerous as it gives lower priority to a group who have greater need and also who may already be subject to discrimination.

The dignity of the human person, as reinforced by the preferential option for the poor, would give older people and those with chronic conditions a higher priority. Notwithstanding the need to acknowledge mortality and the limits of medicine, it is important to resist any attitude which would devalue the lives of older people. Some interventions may be less effective for older people, but this determination should be made on the basis of the person's health and not on their age or the expected number of years they may have left according to a mortality table.

Pope Benedict XVI on his recent visit to Britain reaffirmed the Church's respect for the elderly. When visiting St Peter's Residence, a residential home for the elderly in Vauxhall, London, he said, 'For her part the Church has always had great respect for the elderly... God wills a proper respect for the dignity and worth, the health and well-being of the elderly and through her charitable institutions in Britain... the Church seeks to fulfill the Lord's command to respect life, regardless of *age* or circumstances.'

Are there other systemic kinds of discrimination that occur in healthcare allocation?

There are other groups that are likely to face discrimination in the allocation of healthcare resources, either because they are not as vocal and articulate as other groups - particularly those who have no one to speak for them - or because of social exclusion, or because they are not deemed to have a high quality of life. This will include people with mental impairment, both the mentally ill and those with learning disabilities. It will include prisoners, immigrants and those deemed responsible for their condition (for example, because of substance misuse). Concern with the most marginalised expresses directly the Spirit of the Gospel.

There is a real danger that as the problem of allocation becomes more acute this will be used to justify forms of discrimination. In relation to some groups such as immigrants this may involve abandonment. Already there are voices calling even for the killing of people with dementia. Neither abandonment nor intentional killing are compatible with human dignity, the foundational principle of Catholic social teaching.

Some discrimination is intentional, but other forms are the result of thoughtlessness. In general these forms of discrimination are best resisted by identifying them. Unidentified inequality cannot be redressed.

Does everyone have a right to healthcare?

From the perspective of Catholic social teaching there is a right to healthcare as there is a right to have access to other basic human goods within society. This right is rooted in solidarity and the conception of the common good. As John XXII argued, 'it is generally accepted today that the common good is best safeguarded when personal rights and duties are guaranteed' (1963: 60). Nevertheless, the language of 'rights' is sometimes used in a problematic way as though rights could exist without responsibilities. In the perspective of Catholic social teaching rights are understood in relation to the common good and to human flourishing. There is a right to healthcare, and like all human rights, this is rooted in dignity of the human person. It is a right of access to a reasonable level of healthcare in the context of the resources of society.

Does a right to healthcare imply that the state should deliver healthcare?

No. Other human goods to which people have a right - housing, food, employment, a living wage, social care - are safeguarded by society but are not exclusively provided by the state. Typically the state steps in as a safety-net when private provision fails. In the United Kingdom the state is currently the primary provider of education and healthcare. This is not the case in all other countries and it was not the case in the United Kingdom before the twentieth century. The National Health Service has proved a popular model of provision, but it is important to note that this is not the only way to ensure healthcare provision. The current mix of state, private and charitable funding may alter and the system may see a shift towards state commissioning and funding with private delivery, as is common in France. Catholic social teaching is neither opposed in principle nor committed to any one model of delivery, but what is essential is that delivery embodies both an efficient use of resources and a fair distribution according to healthcare needs and in relation to other social priorities.

The White Paper with its distinction between 'commissioning' and 'providing' marks a move away from the assumption that the state will or should be the universal deliverer of healthcare. The NHS will continue to commission and pay for services, but not necessarily to deliver them. This may generate efficiencies and may bring down costs but it may also lead to greater diversity of provisions and hence inequalities. Catholic social teaching is not opposed to this change in principle, but vigilance is needed if the new patterns of delivery are to benefit or at least not to harm those with the greatest healthcare needs.

Must a fair system of healthcare be free at the point of delivery?

No. There seems no reason to require that to be fair a system must be free at the point of delivery. The National Health Service was built on this aspiration but, in fact, it does not apply to prescription medication, glasses or dental treatment. Furthermore, there is good reason to believe that charging can influence behaviour and so reduce waste, for example the waste of missed appointments. Other countries have mixed systems; for example, if a person does not have insurance, emergency services will still be given, but the costs will later be sought if the person has the means to pay. Interestingly even the radical change embodied in the White Paper leaves intact the principle that treatment should be free at the point of delivery. Nevertheless, different methods of charging or covering cost should be distinguished from different degrees of access. The same service could be accessible to all and free at that point and yet the cost could be recovered from a varying mixture of taxation, insurance, direct charging, means tested benefit and charitable donation.

Can a 'two tier' system (where people can choose to pay more for extra services) be a fair system?

The Gospel seems to imply that inequality is not unfair if the needs of the poorest are met (*Matthew* 20.1-16). The message of Jesus is that God's generosity goes beyond the limits of justice, but this point has application to the issue of fairness and allocation. If there is a system that addresses basic need but has more inequality on top of this, this inequality is not unfair so long as it improves the situation of the poorest, that is, the most needy and most vulnerable, in society. From the perspective of Catholic social teaching, if a 'two tier' system enables wider provision then this seems to be a benefit and not an injustice to the poorest.

At what level should decisions be made?

The principle of subsidiarity implies that decisions should be made wherever possible at the lowest level, i.e. at the local level and with the individual practitioner. This is also supported by the idea of professional clinical judgement and the trust needed in the doctor patient relationship. However if doctors are to make decisions then they must make financial judgements in relation to care, which some professionals are uneasy about. Furthermore there is a need for consistency and transparency so as to prevent discrimination. This is much easier if guidelines are set at a higher level, leaving some scope in application to clinicians. Clinicians have a personal responsibility to spend money wisely and not to exercise discretion in ways that produce a cost disproportionate to any clinical benefit that may be secured. Nor need allocation decisions always come from 'above'. While doctors should offer services according to agreed guidelines, patients can consider renouncing what they have a right to, for the sake of those in greater need. My decision whether or not to accept something that has been allocated to me is also an exercise of subsidiarity.

The idea of subsidiarity seems to have influenced the White paper which speaks of the need to 'radically delayer and simplify the number of NHS bodies' and to 'devolve power and responsibility for commissioning services to the healthcare professionals closest to patients'. This is the rationale for giving GPs power and hence responsibility for allocation decisions. Nevertheless, the suspicion must be that in a time of austerity, the government may be seeking to avoid blame (and responsibility) for difficult allocation decisions by giving a lower level body the role of deciding what (not) to fund. This responsibility is in tension with the primarily medical focus of doctors and the need for patients to trust their doctors. National bodies such as the Care Quality Commission and NICE will continue to set standards that GPs will be required to meet. Thus in theory care should not suffer. Nevertheless, the measures used by NICE are themselves problematic, not least the use of QALYs. The principle of subsidiarity requires decisions to be made at the appropriate level and in the right way. This is not always at the lowest possible level.

Must a 'postcode lottery' necessarily be an unfair system?

A lottery need not be unfair but the 'postcode lottery' may well be a biased lottery in which differences are systemic and reflect historical injustices. Variations may also be due to disinvestment - the restriction of some services to pay for the provision of other preferred services. Such decisions may well reflect local politics and the ability of groups to defend their own interests to the disadvantage of others. Nevertheless, variations may also reflect greater local need or may be due to local decision making of a kind justified by subsidiarity. Some inequalities (e.g. those due to the difficulties of transport in rural areas) are difficult to overcome though efforts are made to mitigate them. A postcode lottery is unfair where it is based on underlying inequalities that have not been addressed. The White Paper discusses inequality but its emphasis on local decision making could lead to selective local disinvestment.

Should allocation reflect what a person has paid in?

Fairness in distributing goods can be measured in relation not only to need but also to contribution. This is seen in ideas of a fair wage or a fair price. All other things being equal, it seems unfair if an older person who has contributed financially to the system all his or her life is deprived of treatment in favour of a younger person who has contributed very little. On the other hand, the aim of systems of taxation and insurance is to spread costs so that money is available when it is needed. Furthermore the financial contribution someone has made may depend on unfair inequalities or be compromised by other social contributions. A full time carer may not have been able to take paid work, while some work is highly remunerated even though it is has doubtful benefit to society. Furthermore, the principle of the preferential option for the poor implies that healthcare ought to be allocated *preferentially* to those least able to contribute to it. Reminding people of the contribution made by older people may be helpful in resisting age-related discrimination. However, as a matter of principle, need provides a better criterion for healthcare allocation than that provided by the measure of contribution.

How does the Gospel provide a model for allocation decisions?

Section 2 ended with the suggestion that the criterion for fair allocation decisions should be 'to each as he or she has need'. (*Acts* 4.35) The model suggested for this was Jesus' parable of the Good Samaritan (*Luke* 10.25-37), offering a simple picture of one human being responding to the clear needs of another. In Section 1 it was noted that NICE had attempted to dismiss the needs-based approach to allocation as 'Marxist'. However, one does not have to be a Marxist to see that need is relevant to allocation. It is unfair to discriminate on the basis of race, gender or religion, except where these affect health needs. However, it is fair to discriminate on the basis of need. The aim of allocating healthcare resources is to address people's health needs.

3.4   How can one identify healthcare needs?

Does Catholic social teaching help identify health needs?

Catholic social teaching calls attention to the person in his or her totality: physical, emotional, social, intellectual, and spiritual. It does not provide a specific account of health or healthcare but relates these to the person as a whole. The word 'health' has its roots in the Old English word 'hoelth' meaning wholeness - being whole, sound or well. Failure to recognise this meaning of health can lead to human dignity being undermined.

How do healthcare needs relate to health needs?

Human beings have a need for healthcare because continued life and health are human goods and healthcare promotes and protects these goods. 'Healthcare needs' are requirements for health secured by healthcare. Nevertheless, health is not the only human good and healthcare is not the only activity that secures health. Health also requires adequate food and shelter, hygiene and sanitation, reasonable conditions of work, social care and also education. If these other needs are not met then health may suffer dramatically. Historians point out that public sanitation and adequate nutrition have done more to increase life expectancy in the UK than improvements in medicine. It is still the case that inequalities in health (life expectancy, morbidity) are determined more by wider inequalities in society (in income, housing and education) than they are by unequal access to healthcare. This is a further reason to be cautious before taking money from other areas and putting them into healthcare.

Can healthcare needs be distinguished from wants?

Some healthcare needs can readily be distinguished from wants. If someone requires urgent medical treatment in an accident or emergency situation, and without that treatment the person would die or suffer serious injury, then this is a clear case of a healthcare need. This need is in contrast with the desire for medical treatment, for example elective cosmetic surgery, where even the person seeking the treatment would agree that it was not medically essential. However, the division between 'need' and 'want' is not easy to make, especially in cases where someone could live without treatment but treatment would improve quality of life (for example, a hip replacement). The distinction of need and want is also difficult in relation to procedures where the efficacy is contested (for example complementary therapies).

From a Catholic perspective it is important to stress that procedures which are unjust or unethical (for example, elective abortion) do not meet healthcare needs. In some countries (other than the United Kingdom) there is a stronger distinction between procedures that are tolerated by law and those that are funded by the state. In the context of limited resources it is doubly unjust to spend money on abortion or the destructive use of human embryos.

Can healthcare needs be distinguished from social care needs?

Within Catholic thought, healthcare includes medical care and basic nursing care but is distinguished from social care. Health care relates immediately to the goods of life and physical and mental health, as these can be secured by means such as medicine and surgery. Social care involves support and care of a non-medical kind aimed towards helping people flourish in the social environment. Nevertheless, there are areas of overlap, for example where people have social care needs as a result of disease, as with dementia. For historical reasons in the United Kingdom healthcare and social care are funded and delivered in very different ways. The difference between these two patterns of allocation leads to patients with different conditions experiencing very different levels of care, which raises a question of fairness. On the other hand the rising cost of social care makes it difficult to envisage a system of social care free for everyone at the point of delivery. Fairness across health and social care therefore seems to require asking radical questions about the model of providing healthcare free at the point of delivery.

How does healthcare need relate to the QALY?

As outlined in Section 1, an important measure of the need for healthcare, used by health economists, is the Quality Adjusted Life Year (QALY). This effectively identifies healthcare need with someone's capacity to benefit (how much long term benefit the intervention will give). Capacity to benefit is clearly an aspect of need. If a treatment would not benefit someone at all then they cannot be said to need it. However, capacity to benefit is only one aspect of need. For example, it does not take into account the urgency of the need or the extent of the person's present suffering. For this reason, even the utilitarian philosopher John Harris has argued that 'the need for health care cannot legitimately be equated exclusively with *one* measure of the degree to which health care can benefit the individual'. QALYs generate a systemic bias against the elderly and against those with disability or complex co-morbidities and are difficult to reconcile with Catholic social teaching.

Can QALYs be used in conjunction with social value judgements?

As stated above (Section 1) NICE has recognised that allocation decisions reflect social value judgements both as to the weighting of quality of life and as to the balancing of utility and fairness. Hence NICE has used public consultation and its Citizen's Council to help it make socially responsible decisions. However, these mechanisms do little to offset the systematic bias inherent in QALYs against older patients and those with disabilities. This problem may also be traced to a deeper one: seeing the final goal of healthcare not as addressing the healthcare needs of individual citizens but as maximizing health benefit to the population as a whole. Unless these defects are remedied the inclusion of social value judgements will remain an afterthought in a process determined by an unfair utilitarian measure.

What aspects should be considered when assessing healthcare need?

Capacity to benefit (measured by the QALY) measures one aspect of need but it is not the only measure of need. Fisher and Gormally mention ten measures of need: (1) greater urgency, (2) greater likelihood to benefit, (3) likelihood of greater benefit, (4) likelihood of lesser burden from treatment, (5) lesser likelihood of harm from treatment, (6) likelihood of greater harm without treatment, (7) likelihood to gain the same benefit from less treatment, (8) likelihood to need less treatment, (9) lack of alternative methods to satisfy need, and (10) greater likelihood to infect others if untreated (2001: 129). We might also measure need by reference to the kind of intervention that is needed. Feeding, for example, is a more basic activity and more fundamental expression of solidarity than giving medicine. If someone can benefit from food and fluids then these needs seem to have a priority over medical treatment, all other things being equal. Defining healthcare and thence identifying healthcare need are clearly complex tasks which require taking many factors into account.

3.5 Who has responsibility for fair healthcare allocation?

Who has primary responsibility for health?

From a Catholic perspective, the primary responsibility for an adult's health lies with that person. Health is a gift to that person from God, and good health is also important in order to fulfil our duties towards others. Looking after our health is not the only goal in life, and there are circumstances when we may decide to take serious risks with our lives, but most goals are not best promoted by neglecting to take care of our health. Furthermore, if people neglect their health they will require healthcare which is taken away from others.

It is the responsibility of parents or guardians to care for the health of children and gradually to teach them to take care of themselves. Within the family and among those who live a common life together, the bonds of mutual affection give rise to a proper concern for one another's health. Finally, the government also has a role in ensuring that all citizens have access to affordable medical care. As responsibility for health begins with each person, it is not unfair if the system incentivises responsible behaviour. There seems to be an echo of this in 2 Thessalonians 3.10. If a person can feed themselves then it is unfair for them to depend on the common purse.

How should allocation reflect personal responsibility?

The dignity of the human person in Catholic teaching implies both rights and responsibilities. If health is primarily a responsibility of the individual, then it is reasonable for a system to incentivise responsible behaviour and to disincentivise irresponsible behaviour. This currently happens in relation to some interventions and behaviours that reduce their effectiveness. If a person cannot stop drinking for six months they may be denied a liver transplant, as the transplant is unlikely to be effective unless the person's behaviour also changes. Many public health interventions mix incentives and disincentives, for example by increasing the tax on cigarettes and reducing the places where it is possible to smoke.

In relation to healthcare there are dangers here in relation to discrimination and judgmental attitudes, especially in cases where, for example, someone suffers from past behaviour when the risks were less evident. It is also the case that it is easier for people to take responsibility if they are more affluent and have a variety of choices in life and better education. Tying healthcare too closely to 'responsible behaviour' risks further marginalising the poorest in society. Nevertheless, responsibility does lie with the person and encouraging responsibility is an expression of respect for the person.

Is it dishonest for professionals to frame options by reference to what is affordable?

One feature of current practice is that when patients are presented with 'options' these are already limited by financial considerations. Treatments that are not affordable are not presented as options. This does not seem dishonest if it reflects the limits of what is available to the doctor. However, if this framing is influenced by a judgment that a certain treatment which would be available to one patient is not being offered to a different patient then this judgement must be made by defensible clinical criteria and should ideally be related to agreed policies. Making policies explicit helps determine whether they are fair or whether they involve unfair discrimination. If the framing of options is done in this way then the professional will be able to explain, if challenged, why a particular treatment was not indicated for this patient.

Is the issue of allocation primarily a matter for individual professionals?

While this booklet is aimed at professionals working in the National Health Service, allocation issues are often decided at a higher level with the setting of budgets and targets. In this respect the issue of allocation has already had a profound effect on structures and on the scope for individual professional judgement, which is more limited than in the past. Nevertheless, the professional can react to these targets and should raise the issue where target-setting seems to have a harmful effect on patients, secure in the knowledge that this will not adversely affect their future career. To alert managers to safety issues is a duty of professionals (see for example General Medical Council 2010). Nevertheless, the scope for individual action may be limited. If responsibility for commissioning is devolved to professionals then there will be some power to make efficiency savings and to decide sometimes to spend more on a particular treatment, but with budgets under strain the scope for action will still be very limited. For all the government uses the language of choice, when choices involve costs then choices will generally be constrained.

How should politicians act justly and responsibly in relation to healthcare allocation?

It is often at the political level that strategic decisions are made about healthcare allocation. Such decisions concern not only the overall size of budgets but also the setting of key targets, the re-organisation of structures in the health service and such matters as the centralising or decentralising of services and the opening, closing or building of hospitals or service centres. The re-organisation of the health service is costly on many levels, not least the opportunity cost of investing time and effort into making the change. This is an immediate cost of the kind of radical change envisaged in the White Paper. Even if it saves money in the long run it costs money in the short term and the health service has suffered from a great number of such short term re-organisational costs, without having time to reap the alleged benefits of one or other system. The challenge for politicians is to resist pressure to make such decisions on the basis of immediate political gain rather than on the basis of the common good. This is true at any time but especially so when decisions must be made to restrict or reduce services in a particular area. The danger here, as mentioned already, is that a devolution of decision making is the excuse for avoiding responsibility for difficult decisions.

How should regulators act justly and responsibly in relation to healthcare allocation?

Regulators such as NICE should seek measures of costs effectiveness and efficiency which are related to need and which do not entrench systemic discrimination. The agreement to incorporate within its next edition of *Social Value Judgements* the need to take into account 'severity of disease' in its decision taking is to be welcomed, although the effect of this is as yet unknown.

From this perspective the continued use of the QALY is something that must be reviewed. QALY analysis may be useful for comparing technologies to treat the same condition. However, it does not provide a fair means for comparing treatments offered to different patient groups. Consideration of equity or justice must take priority over QALY comparisons where treatments concern older patients or those with disabilities. Most fundamentally, regulators should measure effectiveness in relation to health need which, as set out above, has a number of aspects, of which ability to benefit is only one. Finally, as argued in Section 1, decisions around cost-effectiveness should be made in the context of the realistic prospective budget of the health service and with a recognition of who is likely to lose out if a more expensive technology is approved.

How should someone who has responsibility for commissioning practices that are legal and desired but which are not needs discharge this responsibility?

The issue of commissioning desired but unnecessary services may create difficulties of conscience for the person responsible for the commissioning. This may be because the desired services are unethical, or because they are of doubtful effectiveness. Such matters are complicated where there is disagreement about whether the service is unethical (as with abortion) or whether it is ineffective (as with acupuncture). In such a situation, the role may require the agreeing of a set of proposals that include some which are objectionable. This is a classic case of 'co-operation' where a person might co-operate in the process for the sake of the good that comes out of it, despite the fact that it involves enabling some objectionable practices. In general, a person should resist commissioning services that he or she thinks would be harmful, wasteful, or unethical but the scope for resistance may be limited.

How might allocation pressures affect the right of professionals to conscientiously-object to unethical procedures?

In principle, pressure on resources should not affect the right of professionals to conscientiously object to practices they regard as unethical. However, in practice pressure on resources make it difficult for organisations both to provide a full range of legal services and fully to respect the conscience of professionals who object to acting unethically in the field of medicine.

In principle, a physician should be supported in his or her objection, for example, to providing abortion. The right to object to this 'service' is based on the aims of the profession and the duty to protect the patient from harm (in this case the harm of a deliberate miscarriage). However, asserting this right is made complicated by the fact that some such procedures are socially accepted and state funded.

The law and the medical profession recognise a limited right of a doctor or pharmacist to conscientiously object. However, this recognition is unfortunately defective in that it is frequently based only on the right to freedom in personal opinions, rather than on a right to object for the sake of patients and the common good. Hence the patient's alleged right to access services is believed to trump the professional's right of conscience, even where the professional has reason to believe these 'services' would be detrimental. In the context of increasing pressure to deliver efficiently against targets, it will be harder to protect those professionals who object to providing services. Yet it is in the interest of professionals, patients and society to defend a robust right of conscientious objection.

Is it unfair to exclude some patients from treatment altogether?

In any healthcare system there is some cut off in providing ever more expensive treatments for ever more marginal benefit. However, this will mean that at a certain point a decision is taken not to provide this treatment for a particular patient due to cost. This situation may be disguised by framing the options available, or by a system of queuing, but it already occurs. The situation is more difficult when there is no other treatment available or when there is a serious risk of death. In general, efforts should be made not to leave a patient with no hope, but in some cases they will reach the limit of what is possible with affordable medicine. It is essential in every case that no patient is abandoned. Priority should be given to providing everyone with basic care, shelter, nutrition, hydration and nursing care and analgesia where needed. Limits on treatment do not equate to limits on care.

What can be done within the available resources to improve quality of care?

There is widespread agreement that a great deal can be done to improve quality of care without increasing spending. A key element is respect for the dignity of the person as expressed in an ethos of care. The culture of targets has solved some problems, for example long waiting lists, but it can be in tension with the care of the whole person. Despite the great advances in medical knowledge, healthcare is still labour intensive and therefore efforts to increase quality within resource constraints must involve efforts to recruit, train and support staff appropriately, especially the least well paid staff who have most contact with patients, the healthcare assistants.

Summary Conclusion

In summary, difficult allocation decisions are inevitable and should be faced honestly. The fact that it is not possible to realise every possible health benefit does not mean that we should not seek to allocate in accordance to need. Rather, need is a central category for allocation. Fair allocation will focus on allocating to each according to need and prioritising those in greatest need. The key requirement is to ration fairly and to respect the human dignity of every person, especially the most vulnerable.

Bibliography

Age Concern. 2005. *'Age Concern's response to NICE's consultation on Social Value Judgements'*.

Ashley, B.M. and K.D. O'Rourke. 1994. *Ethics of Health Care: An Introductory Textbook.* Washington: Georgetown University Press.

Bartley, M. 2004. *Health Inequality.* Cambridge: Polity.

BBC. 2010. *'Hospitals to face financial penalties for readmissions,'* at http://news.bbc.co.uk/1/hi/health/10262344.stm

BBC.2010. *'Nice to lose powers to decide on new drugs,'* at http://www.bbc.co.uk/news/health-11664684?print-true

Beck, A. 2008. *Dorothy Day.* London: CTS.

Benedict XVI, 2009. *Caritas in Veritate.*

Bishops of England and Wales, 1996. *The Common Good.*

Bishops of England and Wales. 2008. *Mission of the Church to Migrants in England and Wales.* London: CTS.

BMA. 2010. *Equity and excellence; Liberating the NHS.* BMA Response. http://web2.bma.org.uk/pressrel.nsf/wlu/SGOY-89RFAJ?OpenDocument&vw=wfms.

Boots. 2010. *'Regulator to lose drug funding powers'*, at http://www.webmd.boots.com.news/20101031/

Brock D.W. 2003. *'Cost Effectiveness and Priority Setting,'* pp.3-5, at http://www.bioethics.nih.gov/research/ehpolicy/prioritysetting.pdf

Callahan D. 1990. *What Kind of Life: the Limits of Medical Progress.* Washington: Georgetown University Press.

Christian Institute. 19th September 2008. *'Baroness Warnock says elderly have "duty to die"'*(from *'Life and Work'* of Church of Scotland).

Compendium of the Social Doctrine of the Church. London: Continuum 2005.

Day, D. 1997. *The Long Loneliness.* San Francisco: Harper Collins.

Department of Health News Releases 2000. *Maximising Value For Money In The NHS.*

Department of Health Departmental Report. 2006.

Department of Health. 2010. *Equity and excellence: Liberating the NHS.*

Dwyer, J.A. 1994. *'Healthcare'*, in *The New Dictionary of Catholic Social Thought.* Collegeville: Liturgical Press.

Fisher, A. and L. Gormally, 2001. *Healthcare Allocation: An Ethical Framework for Public Policy.* London: Linacre Centre.

Gately, P. 2008. *Perceptions of Personhood and Healthcare Allocation,* Unpublished MA thesis, St Mary's University College, Twickenham.

Guardian. 2010. *'NICE to lose powers to decide on new drugs',* at http://www.guardian.co.uk/politics/2010/oct/29/

Hardwig, J. 2000. *'Is There a Duty to Die?'* in P. Singer and H. Kuhse (eds.) 2000. *Bioethics: An Anthology.* Oxford: Blackwell Publishers.

House of Commons Health Committee. 2007. *National Institute of Health and Clinical Excellence; First Report of Session 2007-08, Volume 1 - 239-240.*

John XXIII, 1963. *Pacem in Terris.*

John Paul II, 1987. *Sollicitudo Rei Socialis.*

John Paul II, 1991. *Centesimus Annus.*

John Paul II, 1995. *Evangelium Vitae.*

Joint Committee on Human Rights. 2007. Eighteenth Report Session 2006-07.

Jones, D.A. 2009. *'Incapacity and personhood: respecting the non-autonomous self'* in H. Watt (ed.) 2009. *Incapacity & Care: Moral problems in healthcare and research.* London: The Linacre Centre.

Jones, D.A. 2010. *'The End of Bioethics?',* *The Pastoral Review* January/February.

Leo XIII, 1891. *Rerum Novarum.*

National Institute for Health and Clinical Excellence. 2005. *Social Value Judgements - Principles for the development of NICE guidance.*

National Institute for Health and Clinical Excellence. 2008. *Social Value Judgements, Second Edition.*

National Institute for Health and Clinical Excellence. *'Threshold workshop',* at http://www.nice.org.uk

Nuffield Trust. *Funding and Performance of Healthcare Systems in the Four Countries of the UK Before and After Devolution,* at www.nuffieldtrust.org.uk

Office of National Statistics. 2009. 2008-based Population projections, at http://www.ons.gov.uk

Overall, C. 2003. *Aging, Death and Human Longevity: A Philosophical Enquiry.* Berkeley: University of California Press.

Paul VI, 1971. *Octagesima Adveniens.*

Pontifical Council for the Pontifical Care of Migrants and Itinerant People. 2004. *Instruction Erga Migrantes Caritas Christi.* Rome: Vatican Press.

Reeves, R. 2000. *Fair Treatment: public conceptions of distributive justice in healthcare.* Unpublished D. Phil thesis, University of Oxford.

Bibliography

Sass, H. M. 1995. '*The New Triad: Responsibility, Solidarity and Subsidiarity*', *Journal of Medicine and Philosophy* 20: 587-594.

United States Catholic Conference (USCC). 1981. *Health and Healthcare: A Pastoral Letter of the American Bishops.* Washington, DC: United States Catholic Conference.

Second Vatican Council. 1965. *Gaudium et Spes.*

UNISON. 2010. *More than Just a Brand.* http://www.unison.org.uk/acrobat/19460.pdf.

Williams, A. 1997. '*The rationing debate: Rationing healthcare by age; The case for*', pp. 2-3 on http://www.bmj.com/cgi/contents/full/314/7083/820